# OCR

## AS/A LEVEL

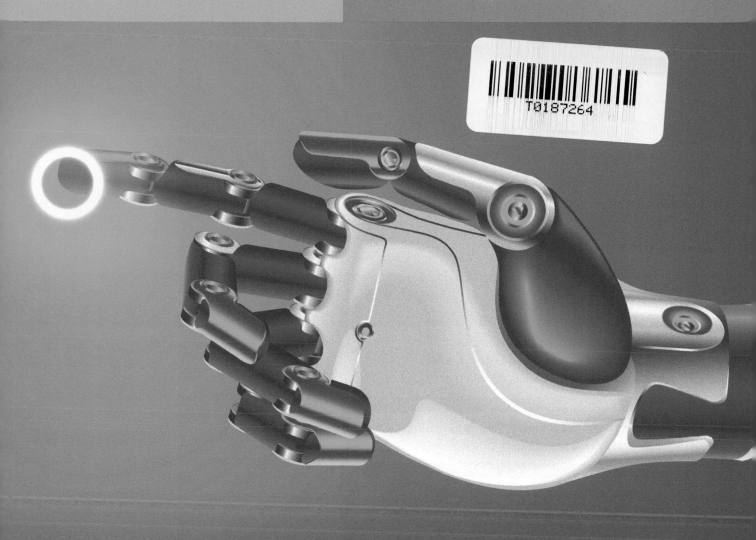

# WORKBOOK

# Computer Science 2

## Algorithms and programming

Sarah Lawrey

HODDER EDUCATION
LEARN MORE

# Contents

**WORKBOOK**

**(1)** This workbook will help you to prepare for the **Computer Science Algorithms and programming** exams.

**(2)** Content highlighted with a red bar is for the full A level only and is not needed for the AS.

**(3)** Your **exam** will include a range of questions requiring short and long responses. You will also have extended response questions.

**(4)** For **each topic** of the exam there are:
- stimulus materials including key terms and concepts
- short-answer questions that build up to exam-style questions
- space for you to write or plan your answers.

**(5)** **Answering the questions** will help you to build your skills and meet the assessment objectives AO1 (Demonstrate knowledge and understanding), AO2 (Apply knowledge and understanding), AO3 (Design, program and evaluate computer systems).

**(6)** You still need to read your textbook and refer to your revision guides and lesson notes.

**(7)** Marks available are indicated for all questions so that you can gauge the level of detail required in your answers.

**(8)** Timings are given for the exam-style questions to make your practice as realistic as possible.

**(9)** Answers are available at:
**www.hoddereducation.co.uk/workbookanswers**

# Elements of computational thinking

## Thinking abstractly

Computational thinking requires abstraction. It requires us to sort out what is and isn't immediately important to the part of the problem that we are trying to solve. Abstraction is used in our daily lives to help provide us with the necessary information that we require, and remove the detail that is not immediately important. A particular example is the London underground map; what tourists and commuters using the underground receive is a simple map of coloured lines to represent each station and route. In actual fact, the underground structure is far more complex and not the network of neat straight lines we see on a typical underground representation. Much of the complexity has been abstracted out to allow the important information to be identified.

If we did not practise abstraction and had all the detail available, all of the time, for a problem we are trying to solve, or a task we are trying to perform, information could prove difficult to decipher. For example, if the underground map that we gave tourists and commuters had the tracks overlapping in exactly the way that they do and all the building and streets in between each and every station, it would be very difficult for our brains to process this chaos.

By abstracting out the detail from a problem, we can understand what is important for that part of the problem. In computer science it helps us to dedicate certain tasks to certain concepts and so abstract out different responsibilities to different parts of a system. An example of this would be the use of layers in protocols. The responsibilities of a protocol in most cases is abstracted into different layers. This mean that each layer is responsible for a different part of the process. The benefit of this is that if something is not working correctly with the protocol, it is possible to locate the layer in which the error is occurring. This narrows down the possibility of what the problem might be.

Abstraction can be described as a representation of reality, but not the whole of the reality itself. It can be thought of as a snapshot of what is important to that problem or task at that time. Another application of abstraction is to identify the parts of a problem that can be pulled out and applied to many other elements of a program. This creates a 'bare bones' structure of a problem that may them be used repeatedly. In programming, examples of this would be classes and objects.

---

**1** Define what is meant by the term 'abstraction'. `2 marks`

................................................................................................................................

................................................................................................................................

................................................................................................................................

................................................................................................................................

**2** Give two examples of how abstraction can be used. `2 marks`

................................................................................................................................

................................................................................................................................

................................................................................................................................

................................................................................................................................

**3** Explain the difference between abstraction and reality. *(2 marks)*

........................................................................................................................................

........................................................................................................................................

........................................................................................................................................

........................................................................................................................................

**4** Explain two benefits of using abstraction to solve problems. *(4 marks)*

........................................................................................................................................

........................................................................................................................................

........................................................................................................................................

........................................................................................................................................

........................................................................................................................................

........................................................................................................................................

**5** Think about giving directions to a person from the centre of your local town to your house. How would you use abstraction in this task? *(3 marks)*

........................................................................................................................................

........................................................................................................................................

........................................................................................................................................

........................................................................................................................................

........................................................................................................................................

........................................................................................................................................

........................................................................................................................................

# Thinking ahead

Thinking ahead means thinking about planning. To create an effective program, we need to think about all the different aspects that it requires. This may involve thinking about other future uses for the code that we create, to allow us to reutilise the code.

If we plan our code carefully and divide the code into reuseable components, this could save us a lot of time and effort in the future. This is because we can return to the code and reuse parts of it when we want a similar function to occur in a different program. One example of thinking ahead in this way is the libraries that are available to use with most programming languages. These are ways that the creators of the programming language have thought ahead and created components that can be reused by many people over and over again.

Another part of thinking ahead is determining the inputs and outputs of a program. One of the main reasons we use computers is to give the computer an input in search of a certain output. Therefore, when creating a program, we need to think of all the things that could be input into the program and make sure that this will give us all the correct and desired outputs. If we do not think ahead and plan effectively for each input that is required, then we may not end up with the correct or desired output, which would mean our program is not effective.

The notion of thinking ahead is something that is used in the process of caching. A cache is a place where data is temporarily stored so that it can be accessed more quickly than if it were stored in RAM. The kind of data and instructions that are stored in cache are the ones that are anticipated to be the ones that the computer will need most often. This means that they can be accessed as quickly as possible for repeated use. However, the cache needs to be a suitable size. If a cache is too large, the computer will need to search through too many instructions and data to find what it needs, making the process counterproductive.

If we do not use the skill of thinking ahead when creating programs, we may find that our programs are not very future-proof. They may be fit for the current purpose that we have created them for, but they may not have many reusable components that could save us time in the future, or allow us to input future actions that may be required for a certain output.

**6** Why is the action of thinking ahead important? 2 marks

..........................................................................................................................................................................

..........................................................................................................................................................................

..........................................................................................................................................................................

..........................................................................................................................................................................

..........................................................................................................................................................................

**7** Why is it important to identify the correct inputs and outputs? 2 marks

..........................................................................................................................................................................

..........................................................................................................................................................................

..........................................................................................................................................................................

..........................................................................................................................................................................

..........................................................................................................................................................................

**8** How are libraries an example of thinking ahead? 2 marks

..........................................................................................................................................................................

..........................................................................................................................................................................

..........................................................................................................................................................................

..........................................................................................................................................................................

..........................................................................................................................................................................

**9** How is the process of caching related to thinking ahead? 2 marks

..........................................................................................................................................................................

..........................................................................................................................................................................

..........................................................................................................................................................................

..........................................................................................................................................................................

..........................................................................................................................................................................

# Thinking procedurally

In order to establish the sequence of instructions needed to solve a problem, it is important to break down the problem into its component parts. This is called 'decomposing the problem'. The component parts that the problem is broken down into are often referred to as the modules of the program. A programmer can then look to program each of these modules in turn. The modules will then be set to interact in order to create the whole system. By breaking the problem down into individual modules, it makes the problem easier to solve. It also means that the modules can be reused in future for other problems that they may be applicable for.

Thinking procedurally means thinking about the sequence in which the component parts need to be ordered to get the correct output or result for the problem. There may be a single, set order that the modules must be given to solve the problem, or there may be a number of ways that the modules can be ordered to solve the problem. This will entirely depend on the nature of the problem. The order that the modules are given may also affect the efficiency of the solution. If we think about the example of making a cup of tea, we can look at how thinking procedurally can apply to this. There are a number of actions that we need to carry out when we make a cup of tea, such as:

- get cup from cupboard
- fill kettle with water
- boil kettle
- put teabag in cup
- add milk

If we look at some of these actions, we can see that the order does matter in some cases, we can't put the teabag in the cup until we have got the cup from the cupboard. We can't boil the kettle until we have filled the kettle with water. However, there are some actions where the order is changeable; for example, once we have got the cup from the cupboard, the order in which we add the boiling water, the milk and the teabag can be changed, and the same result may still be achieved. We can also look at some of the actions and improve the efficiency to achieve the solution. For example, whilst the kettle is boiling, we could get the cup out of the cupboard, add the teabag and add the milk.

---

**10** **What does it mean to think procedurally?**　　　　　　　`2 marks`

.......................................................................................................................................................

.......................................................................................................................................................

.......................................................................................................................................................

.......................................................................................................................................................

**11** **What needs to be done first in order to think about the sequence of a program?**　　`1 mark`

.......................................................................................................................................................

.......................................................................................................................................................

**12** **Why is thinking procedurally an important part of creating a program?**　　`2 marks`

.......................................................................................................................................................

.......................................................................................................................................................

.......................................................................................................................................................

.......................................................................................................................................................

# Thinking logically

In our daily lives, we make thousands of decisions about the different actions we take. It is logic and experience that allow us to make these decisions. We naturally identify where a decision needs to be made and use logic, reasoning and experience to make the decision. The outcome of the decision that we make can often affect our actions in the future and our response to that certain decision if encountered again.

For computers to have the ability to make decisions, we need to identify the points in a program where those decisions will need to be made. We can then decide what possible outcomes there could be as a result of each decision and include this information in the program.

Decision-making in a program is called selection. There are normally two structures that can be used for selection, these are IF ... THEN ... ELSE and CASE ... OF ... ENDCASE. Each structure will be dependent on certain conditions. There is also an element of decision-making in some iteration also. If the iteration is based on a condition loop, it will need to check against the condition set in each iteration and make a decision about whether the condition is fulfilled.

To identify the points in a program where a decision needs to be taken, we need to identify all the possible paths to the solution and any conditions that may affect getting there. This will mostly be dependent on the inputs given to the program and the content of the inputs.

**13** **How could you plan the decisions that need to be made in a program?**  `1 mark`

...................................................................................................................................................................

...................................................................................................................................................................

# Thinking concurrently

We often spend large parts of our day multitasking. Many businesses are built around the ability to complete a number of tasks at the same time. The performance of a computer also depends on the ability to multitask. If a computer could only process one instruction at a time, it would run at a much slower pace. Concurrency is used to create the best performance viable for a computer system.

A simple example of concurrency is washing day. Your parent has said that you and your sibling are not allowed to go out to meet your friends until all the washing is washed, dried, ironed and put away. You look and there are four loads of washing to do. If you washed, dried, ironed and put away each load of washing in turn, this would not be making best use of your time, and you and your sibling may never get to see your friends. Therefore, you could think about completing the task using concurrency. You could wash the first load, then put that load in the dryer. Whilst the first load is drying you could be washing the second load. Then when the first load is dry you could be ironing this whilst your sibling is putting it away. In the washer could be the third load and in the dryer could be the second load. One thing to consider is that although it will save you time, there is a lot more to think about at any given time, when completing tasks concurrently.

This same concept can be used when processing instructions in a computer. This process is also referred to as parallel processing.

In business, a common project planning tool highlights where concurrency can take place. This is called a Gantt chart. This will highlight which parts of the project can be completed alongside others and which tasks are dependent on others.

**14** What benefit can you see to a computer using concurrency? `2 marks`

.......................................................................................................................

.......................................................................................................................

.......................................................................................................................

.......................................................................................................................

**15** What drawback can you see to a computer using concurrency? `2 marks`

.......................................................................................................................

.......................................................................................................................

.......................................................................................................................

.......................................................................................................................

**(20)**

## Exam-style questions

**16** Companies often have large-scale problems that require a computer-based solution. It can be a complex process to create the solution, so computational methods can be applied to make the process easier.

Two of these computational methods are decomposition and abstraction.

**a** Explain what is meant by decomposition and abstraction. `2 marks`

Decomposition:

.......................................................................................................................

.......................................................................................................................

Abstraction:

.......................................................................................................................

.......................................................................................................................

**b** Identify one other computational method. `1 mark`

.......................................................................................................................

**17** An airline company is creating a computer simulation to help train its pilots to fly a new type of aircraft they have purchased. Explain how abstraction can be used in creating the flight simulation program. `4 marks`

.......................................................................................................................

.......................................................................................................................

.......................................................................................................................

.......................................................................................................................

.......................................................................................................................

.......................................................................................................................

**18** Explain how a computer makes use of the process of concurrency. `4 marks`

**19** Give one advantage and one disadvantage of using computational methods to decide what to have for dinner. `2 marks`

**20** Explain how pipelining can be used to improve the efficiency of an assembly line for a car manufacturer. `4 marks`

**21** Victoria creates a website that provides video tutorials about gardening. She is looking at several companies that can host her website. Some of the companies offer caching facilities. Define what is meant by caching and explain how this could be beneficial for Victoria. `4 marks`

# Problem solving and programming

## Programming techniques

There are three basic concepts that programming is based upon; these are sequence, iteration and branching. Branching is often also known as selection. All computer programs are written using these three constructs.

## Sequence

Sequence refers to the order in which the instructions are carried out. Sometimes, there is only one sequence in which the instructions can be carried out to achieve the correct result. Sometimes, there can be several different sequences that can be used to carry out the instructions and all of them will achieve the correct result. If the correct sequence is not established for a program, this may create a logical error.

## Iteration

Iteration refers to the repetition of parts of a program. This may be in the form of a loop (counting or conditional). Recursion is a type of iteration where a subroutine can be set to call itself to create the repetition.

## Branching

Branching refers to a point in a program where a decision is made about which path through the program is to be followed. This will often depend on a condition being met or not being met. The program will branch to whichever part is required, based upon the outcome of the conditional test.

---

**1** State whether a FOR ... NEXT command is an example of sequence, iteration or branching. **1 mark**

.................................................................................................................................

.................................................................................................................................

**2** Describe the difference between a conditional loop and a count-controlled loop. **2 marks**

.................................................................................................................................

.................................................................................................................................

.................................................................................................................................

.................................................................................................................................

**3** Describe how branching is created in a program. **3 marks**

.................................................................................................................................

.................................................................................................................................

.................................................................................................................................

.................................................................................................................................

.................................................................................................................................

**4** What can be used to replace tail recursion? **1 mark**

.................................................................................................................................

.................................................................................................................................

**5** What three elements must be present in a recursive algorithm? `3 marks`

...................................................................................................................................................

...................................................................................................................................................

...................................................................................................................................................

**6** What will happen in a recursive algorithm if a terminating condition is not created? `2 marks`

...................................................................................................................................................

...................................................................................................................................................

...................................................................................................................................................

## Variables

A variable is a named location in which a value is stored. This value can be changed at any time, by assigning a new value, during the running of the program. A variable is given a data type to tell the program what kind of data is stored.

There are two different types of variable: global and local. A global variable is one that is declared outside a subroutine. This type of variable is visible to the whole program and can be accessed at any time. A local variable is one that is declared within a subroutine and can only be accessed when that subroutine is called.

**7** What is the difference between a global and a local variable? `2 marks`

...................................................................................................................................................

...................................................................................................................................................

...................................................................................................................................................

...................................................................................................................................................

**8** Why is it good practice to use local variables where possible? `1 mark`

...................................................................................................................................................

...................................................................................................................................................

**9** When would it be suitable to use a global variable? `1 mark`

...................................................................................................................................................

...................................................................................................................................................

## Subroutines

When writing programs is it is often beneficial to separate the program into several modules. This is a form of decomposition. Abstraction can then be used to establish the component parts of each module. This makes it much easier to write and test the program. Modules are also referred to as subroutines or subprograms.

Two types of subroutine are functions and procedures. A function is a self-contained section of a program that is designed to return a value. A sequence of instructions is carried out to create the value that is returned. A procedure is a self-contained section of a program that is a defined set of instructions designed to perform a task. For example, a procedure could be written to sort a set of values.

Many high-level programming languages have in-built functions. You have probably used them many times. An example of an in-built function in Python is the input() command. Each subroutine has a label, for example INPUT. This label is then used to call the subroutine.

When you write a subroutine, you will usually need to feed some data into the subroutine for the program to use. This data is called a parameter and when it is fed into the subroutine it is called 'passing it a parameter'. The parameter will be previously declared as a variable in the program. Several parameters can be passed into a program at a time, if required.

Parameters can be passed using one of two methods. The methods that can be used are passing by value and passing by reference. When a parameter is passed by value, it is only a copy of the variable that is passed to the subroutine. This means that wherever the variable occurs outside the subroutine, the value stored there will not be changed. This is the case even if the value passed is changed within the subroutine. When a parameter is passed by reference, the address of the variable is passed to the subroutine. This means that if the value from the parameter is changed within the subroutine, the value stored elsewhere within the variable will also change.

**10** **What are two benefits of separating a program into modules?**  `2 marks`

.................................................................................................................................

.................................................................................................................................

.................................................................................................................................

.................................................................................................................................

.................................................................................................................................

**11** **What is the difference between a function and a procedure?**  `2 marks`

.................................................................................................................................

.................................................................................................................................

.................................................................................................................................

.................................................................................................................................

.................................................................................................................................

**12** **What is a parameter?**  `1 mark`

.................................................................................................................................

.................................................................................................................................

**13** **What is the difference between passing a parameter by value and passing a parameter by reference?**  `2 marks`

.................................................................................................................................

.................................................................................................................................

.................................................................................................................................

.................................................................................................................................

.................................................................................................................................

# IDE

An Integrated Development Environment (IDE) is often used to write computer programs. An IDE can have many useful tools to help a programmer. These include:

- an editor, to allow the programmer to type the source code
- a debugger, to allow a programmer to test and find errors in the program
- a translator, to allow the program to be translated into machine code
- pretty printing, to allow the programmer to see if they have the correct command words
- auto-completion, to speed up the rate at which the programmer creates the program.

All these tools help the programmer create the program and improve the speed at which they can do this.

**14** **How can an IDE help a programmer develop and debug a program?** `2 marks`

.........................................................................................................................................................

.........................................................................................................................................................

.........................................................................................................................................................

.........................................................................................................................................................

# Object-oriented programming

Object-oriented programming (OOP) is a type of programming paradigm. In OOP, a solution to a problem is created through the development of objects. There are several elements to OOP: classes, methods, attributes, inheritance, encapsulation and polymorphism. OOP focuses on the development of objects rather than actions. It focuses on incorporating both data and processes, rather than treating them as separate elements.

Each object is based on a class. A class is a template that defines the attributes and methods for the object. Once created, an object needs to be initialised. This means that all the attributes need to be given their initial data. An object is initialised using a constructor.

## Encapsulation

Encapsulation is the act of incorporating the data and processes together. A class is an example of encapsulation. The use of get and set methods to access, amend and return data is also an example of encapsulation. One of the reasons data is encapsulated is to make sure that it cannot be accidentally changed. To create encapsulation, an attribute is normally defined as private. This means that the attribute can only be accessed by methods within that class.

## Classes

Often, a system will require multiple classes. This could involve a parent class that contains the information that is applicable to all objects, then child classes are created that contain more specific information. In most occasions, a child class will inherit the attributes and methods from the parent class. Inheritance allows one class to also have all the attributes and methods from another class.

## Polymorphism

Polymorphism is the ability to create objects differently depending on their data type or class. There are many examples in OOP that fall into the definition of polymorphism. One example would be a method that is defined in a parent class but overridden in a child class, dependent on certain circumstances. This is called overriding. A second example could be a function that will behave in different ways depending on the data type of the parameter that it is passed. It could behave one way if it is passed a string and a different way if it is passed an integer.

**15** What is the purpose of a constructor? [1 mark]

...........................................................................................................................................................................

...........................................................................................................................................................................

**16** a Create a class diagram for a class called 'Animal'.

 i Add some suitable attributes to the class diagram, such as height, weight etc. [1 mark]

 ii Add some suitable methods to the class diagram. Think about encapsulating the data. [1 mark]

b **Add two other types of animal to your class diagram.**

   i  Add some suitable attributes to each.

   ii  Add some suitable methods to each.

   iii  Show how the additional classes inherit from the original class.

   iv  Add an example of polymorphism, such as a method overwriting another method.

**17** Write pseudocode to demonstrate a subroutine for one of the get methods that you should have defined in the class diagram.

..........................................................................................................................................................

..........................................................................................................................................................

..........................................................................................................................................................

..........................................................................................................................................................

..........................................................................................................................................................

..........................................................................................................................................................

**18** Write pseudocode to demonstrate a subroutine for one of the set methods that you should have defined in the class diagram.

2 marks

..........................................................................................................................................................

..........................................................................................................................................................

..........................................................................................................................................................

..........................................................................................................................................................

..........................................................................................................................................................

..........................................................................................................................................................

..........................................................................................................................................................

**19** Write pseudocode to demonstrate a constructor for one of the classes that you should have defined in the class diagram.

3 marks

..........................................................................................................................................................

..........................................................................................................................................................

..........................................................................................................................................................

..........................................................................................................................................................

..........................................................................................................................................................

..........................................................................................................................................................

..........................................................................................................................................................

..........................................................................................................................................................

..........................................................................................................................................................

**20** Write pseudocode for the class declaration header of one of the child classes that you should have defined in the class diagram.

1 mark

..........................................................................................................................................................

..........................................................................................................................................................

**21** Write pseudocode to create an object based on the parent class that you should have defined in the class diagram.

`2 marks`

.......................................................................................................................................

.......................................................................................................................................

.......................................................................................................................................

.......................................................................................................................................

.......................................................................................................................................

.......................................................................................................................................

.......................................................................................................................................

## Computational methods

In order to create a computer program to solve a problem, it is important to understand if that problem is solvable by computational methods. One way of deciding if a program is solvable in this way is to test it against the capabilities of a Turing machine. This is a machine that is a mathematical representation of a simple computer. It uses rules and states to determine whether a problem can be solved by computer.

A simple way of looking at whether a problem can be solved using computational methods is to consider whether an algorithm can be created that will solve the problem. Previously, this may have been a more clean-cut decision, but with the development of artificial intelligence and other such technologies, a computer's ability to solve problems is developing into new territory on a regular basis. One thing that may prevent a problem being solvable by computational methods is that we do not have a good enough understanding of the underlying issues of the problem.

To be able to solve a problem, it is important to fully understand what that problem is. Some problems have very complex underlying issues, some may be too challenging to allow the gathering of meaningful data and for some there may not be sufficient data available. If these important factors cannot be recognised in the problem, it may not be possible to create an effective solution.

**22** How can you tell if a problem can be solved by computational methods?

`1 mark`

.......................................................................................................................................

**23** What kind of problem may not be solvable by computational methods?

`1 mark`

.......................................................................................................................................

## Decomposition

An important part of solving a problem is decomposing it into its component parts. When a problem is decomposed, it is much clearer to see what the solution needs to include to be effective. One way of decomposing a problem is to think about the four key elements that it will need to include. These are what:

- the inputs to the program will be
- the outputs from the program will be
- processes will need to occur to achieve the outputs
- data will need to be stored.

These four areas are the fundamental elements of any computer program.

## Top-down design

A common approach to decomposing a problem is the top-down design. This is a hierarchical approach to solving a problem in which modules are highlighted and then structured in a hierarchical fashion, where each module leads into a submodule. This also clearly demonstrates how all parts of the program are related.

This is a simple example of top-down design:

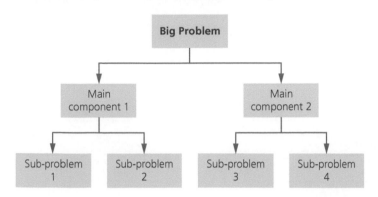

**24** **What is meant by the term 'decomposition'?**  1 mark

.................................................................................................................................

.................................................................................................................................

**25** **Which four key areas is it useful to highlight in problem decomposition?**  4 marks

.................................................................................................................................

.................................................................................................................................

.................................................................................................................................

.................................................................................................................................

.................................................................................................................................

**26** **What benefit can you see for using top-down design?**  1 mark

.................................................................................................................................

.................................................................................................................................

**27** **What drawback can you see for using top-down design?**  2 marks

.................................................................................................................................

.................................................................................................................................

.................................................................................................................................

.................................................................................................................................

**28** **How does decomposition relate to object-oriented programming?**  2 marks

.................................................................................................................................

.................................................................................................................................

.................................................................................................................................

.................................................................................................................................

# Divide and conquer approach

Another approach that can be used in solving certain problems is 'divide and conquer'. In this type of approach, the problem is broken down into the smallest components that it can be, then repeated actions are performed on these components until the desired outcome is received. In other words, the problem is divided (broken down into smallest components) then conquered (actions recursively performed to reach the solution). A typical example of a divide and conquer approach is recursion. Another example of the divide and conquer approach is a binary search. This is a type of searching algorithm that repeatedly divides a set of data until the value required is found. You can learn more about this in the algorithms section.

29 **Can divide and conquer be used to find the Fibonacci sequence? Explain your decision.** 3 marks

.......................................................................................................................................................................

.......................................................................................................................................................................

.......................................................................................................................................................................

.......................................................................................................................................................................

.......................................................................................................................................................................

.......................................................................................................................................................................

# Abstraction

As discussed in the *Thinking abstractly* section, abstraction is also used in computational thinking. It allows us to draw out the relevant detail to the immediate problem that needs solving and remove the detail that isn't necessary at that stage. When decomposition and abstraction are used hand in hand, this creates an effective recipe for solving a problem using computational methods.

# Backtracking

Backtracking is a form of solving problems through the process of trial and error. A backtracking approach solves the first part of a problem, then recursively begins to solve the next part of the problem, based on the first part of the problem. If it reaches a point where it recognises that viable progress cannot be made, it backtracks to the previous stage and then proceeds with a different approach. Backtracking is a natural thought process that we use on a daily basis. Whenever we are making decisions we may think about doing something one way, but then think that wouldn't work, so we think about doing it another way. We use this technique a lot when completing a task such as a crossword. A backtracking algorithm uses recursion and a depth-first approach to solve the problem. The depth-first method is covered in the algorithms section.

A really simple way of looking at the use of backtracking is to think about how you get through a maze. You enter the maze and progress until you get to a point where you can take a different path. You decide which path to take. You keep walking, but you come to a dead end. You then backtrack to where you came from and take a different path. You repeatedly do this until you exit the maze.

**30** How do you think backtracking would apply to solving a sudoku puzzle? `2 marks`

.............................................................................................................................................................

.............................................................................................................................................................

.............................................................................................................................................................

.............................................................................................................................................................

**31** Which two elements are important in the backtracking process? `2 marks`

.............................................................................................................................................................

.............................................................................................................................................................

**32** How do you think backtracking would apply to finding out what is wrong with your computer? `2 marks`

.............................................................................................................................................................

.............................................................................................................................................................

.............................................................................................................................................................

.............................................................................................................................................................

## Data mining

In order to solve some problems a large set of data may be required. This may be because there are a lot of different aspects to consider in order to reach a viable solution. One task in which large data sets are often used is business modelling. Data needs to be input into a system that will allow the model to test every eventuality and outcome that could occur. To analyse large sets of data, a process such as data mining can be used. Data mining is when large sets of data are examined to look for relationships and patterns in the data.

**33** How could a technology company use data mining to find out which new product to develop? `2 marks`

.............................................................................................................................................................

.............................................................................................................................................................

.............................................................................................................................................................

## Heuristic approach

Sometimes when you make decisions, you make them fairly rapidly using 'rule of thumb' thoughts that you have gained from life experiences. We do not have the time to deliberate over all the decisions that we make in a day, so these 'rule of thumb' thoughts are important to our thought processes. They basically allow us to make a shortcut decision on daily aspects in our lives. These are called heuristic thoughts. A heuristic approach can also be used in programming. Rather than a system being designed to follow an algorithm that progresses through a logical process, it may be designed to use 'intelligent guesses' to solve the problem. A very simple example of this could be a file-searching program. One algorithm may search for a file alphabetically until it finds it, whereas a heuristics program may first consider that the file may have been found recently and check the recently accessed file to find it first.

**34** What is a heuristic thought?    1 mark

.................................................................................................................................................

.................................................................................................................................................

**35** How do we use heuristic thoughts in our daily lives?    2 marks

.................................................................................................................................................

.................................................................................................................................................

.................................................................................................................................................

.................................................................................................................................................

**36** How can a heuristic approach be used in programming?    1 mark

.................................................................................................................................................

.................................................................................................................................................

**37** How does heuristics in programming relate to artificial intelligence?    1 mark

.................................................................................................................................................

.................................................................................................................................................

## Performance modelling

It is important to know how well a system will perform in real life before it is implemented. Testing all the possible inputs, processes and outputs a system may need to handle would likely be a very time intensive and exhaustive process. It would also likely be very expensive. For example, if a company was developing a self-driving vehicle, it would be extremely costly to the company to test the vehicle against every different kind of hazard it may encounter. Therefore, performance models can be built that provide a simulated situation and allow many different scenarios to be tested repeatedly. A performance model would also allow scaling up and scaling down of a system to virtually take place in the simulation, so that the company could see what this effect this may have.

**38** What two things could a company save by using a performance model?    2 marks

.................................................................................................................................................

.................................................................................................................................................

.................................................................................................................................................

.................................................................................................................................................

**39** How do you think performance modelling could be used for a network in a company?    2 marks

.................................................................................................................................................

.................................................................................................................................................

.................................................................................................................................................

.................................................................................................................................................

**40** What problems can you see with using performance modelling? `2 marks`

........................................................................................................

........................................................................................................

........................................................................................................

........................................................................................................

## Pipelining

A common computational technique is pipelining. In pipelining, the output of one process becomes the input to the next process. A computer system will have several pipelines and this will allow the computer to process instructions efficiently. Whilst the computer is fetching one instruction in one pipeline, it can be decoding another in a second pipeline and executing another in a third pipeline. This process is also known as parallel processing.

Problems can occur in pipelining when branching is introduced. This may mean that the order in which the instructions need to be carried out can get out of sequence. A pipeline monitoring process is used to make sure the sequence of instructions remains correct and that each pipeline remains full.

**41** How would a computer operate if it could not make use of pipelining? `1 mark`

........................................................................................................

........................................................................................................

**42** How is pipelining used in parallel processing? `2 marks`

........................................................................................................

........................................................................................................

........................................................................................................

........................................................................................................

**43** What are the limitations when using pipelining? `1 mark`

........................................................................................................

........................................................................................................

## Visual representation

It is often easier to consider how a problem can be solved if a visual representation of it is created. A simple example of this would be a graph to represent a trend of a certain aspect. It is easy to see what the trend is by looking at the visual representation of a graph, rather than the data in tabular form. This would be very helpful if it was a large set of data that was being analysed.

**44** How could a visual model show which train routes are used the most on a daily basis? `1 mark`

........................................................................................................

........................................................................................................

# Exam-style questions

**45** A company has a parking meter for its car park. Customers are required to input coins and the expiry time for the ticket is displayed on a screen. The customer pushes a green button when they see the required expiry time for the ticket. Any difference in the coins input compared to the cost of the parking will be given in change. A ticket is then printed to display in the customer's window.

Draw a top-down diagram to represent the parking meter system. **4 marks**

**46** A class has the following criteria:

| monthlyWage |
| --- |
| Name : String |
| Salary : Float |
| Overtime : Float |
| Constructor() |
| getName() |
| getSalary() |
| getOvertime() |
| setName() |
| setSalary() |
| setOvertime() |
| calculateWage() |

a   State the purpose of the Constructor method.

1 mark

b   State the purpose of the getSalary method.

1 mark

c   State the purpose of the setOvertime method.

1 mark

d   All attributes are passed by parameter. All attributes are private. Using
    pseudocode, write a program for the constructor method.

5 marks

**47** Explain what is meant by a divide and conquer approach. Include two examples of
    where it is used in computer science.

5 marks

# Algorithms

Algorithms are the foundation of programming: they are the set of instructions that are created for a system to follow in order to perform a task. There are several ways that an algorithm can be represented; these include structured English, pseudocode and flowcharts. There are several different algorithms that you need to be familiar with.

Certain algorithms are more suitable to certain tasks and one of the skills a programmer needs to develop is deciding which algorithm may be the best to use. Two things that may be considered in this choice are execution time and complexity. Both can affect the efficiency of an algorithm and normally programmers want to try and make an algorithm as efficient as possible.

## Big-O notation

Several methods can be used to determine the efficiency of an algorithm; one method is Big-O notation. Big-O notation describes the worst-case scenario for the efficiency of all or part of an algorithm. It doesn't necessarily look at how fast the algorithm will be executed, but how well it will scale if the data set is increased. There are several states that can be assessed used Big-O notation and these are detailed in the table below.

| Status | Description | Example |
|---|---|---|
| Constant complexity $O(1)$ | Describes an algorithm that will always have the same execution time, regardless of the size of data set. | Pushing data to a stack |
| Linear complexity $O(n)$ | Describes an algorithm that will increase at the same rate in direct proportion to the data set. | A linear search |
| Logarithmic complexity $O(\log n)$ | The rate of increase in the execution time decreases, as the data set increases. This is a very efficient algorithm that will scale well. | Binary search |
| Polynomial complexity $O(n^k)$ | Describes an algorithm where 'n' reflects the size of the input and 'k' reflects a constant value. Not as fast as logarithmic and constant. | Insertion sort, which is $O(n^2)$ |
| Exponential complexity $O(k^n)$ | This type of algorithm scales the worst of all. The execution time grows much faster than any other algorithm. | This is not a status a programmer would strive to have for an algorithm. A possible example could be a brute force algorithm. |

1 **What does Big-O notation measure?** (1 mark)

.......................................................................................................

.......................................................................................................

2 **Which is the slowest growing algorithm status?** (1 mark)

.......................................................................................................

.......................................................................................................

3 **Which is the fastest growing algorithm status?** (1 mark)

.......................................................................................................

.......................................................................................................

4 **Which algorithm status would a bubble sort be?** (1 mark)

.......................................................................................................

.......................................................................................................

# Data structures

Algorithms are also used to create data structures. The algorithm will highlight how data is added to and removed from the data structure. This will be different depending on which data structure is used.

## Stacks

A stack is a data structure that has a last in first out (LIFO) data structure. This means that the last piece of data that is added to the structure is the first piece of data that is removed from the structure. The commands PUSH and POP are often used to add and remove data to a stack. The following algorithm demonstrates how data can be added to a stack:

```
function pushToStack(number)

  indexFirst = 0

  indexLast = 4

  pointerTemp = pointerEnd + 1

  if pointerTemp > indexLast then

    return false

  else

    stack[pointerTemp] = number

    pointerEnd = pointerTemp

    return true

  endif

endfunction
```

---

**5** What is the variable in the brackets on the first line known as?  1 mark

........................................................................................................................................................................................

........................................................................................................................................................................................

**6** Why does the algorithm need to return false in the first conditional check?  1 mark

........................................................................................................................................................................................

........................................................................................................................................................................................

**7** **Write an algorithm in pseudocode that will remove an item of data from the stack.** 4 marks

## Queues

A queue is a data structure that has a first in first out (FIFO) data structure. This means that the first piece of data that is added to the structure is the first piece of data that is removed from the structure. The commands PUSH and POP are often used to add and remove data to a queue. The following algorithm demonstrates how data can be added to a queue:

```
function pushToQueue(number)

  indexFirst = 0

  indexLast = 4

  pointerTemp = pointerEnd + 1

  if pointerTemp > indexLast then

   pointerTemp = indexfirst

  endif

  if pointerTemp == pointerStart then

   return false

  else

  queue[pointerTemp] = number

  pointerEnd = pointerTemp

   return true

  endif

endfunction
```

**8** What is the different between a stack and a queue?    (2 marks)

..................................................................................................................................

..................................................................................................................................

..................................................................................................................................

..................................................................................................................................

**9** Why does the algorithm set the temporary pointer to the first index if the first conditional check is true?    (1 mark)

..................................................................................................................................

..................................................................................................................................

**10** Why does the algorithm perform a check to see if the temporary pointer is equal to the start pointer?    (1 mark)

..................................................................................................................................

..................................................................................................................................

**11** Write an algorithm in pseudocode that will remove an item of data from a queue.    (4 marks)

..................................................................................................................................

..................................................................................................................................

..................................................................................................................................

..................................................................................................................................

..................................................................................................................................

..................................................................................................................................

..................................................................................................................................

..................................................................................................................................

..................................................................................................................................

..................................................................................................................................

..................................................................................................................................

..................................................................................................................................

..................................................................................................................................

..................................................................................................................................

..................................................................................................................................

## Linked lists

A linked list is when new pieces of data are stored in the next available locations and pointers are then used to link the items together in the correct order. A starting pointer indicates where the list begins and then a pointer points to the next item in the list, in the correct sequence. Each item of data in the list is called a node. The last node in the list will have a null pointer.

**12** Add comments to this algorithm to demonstrate your understanding of what it does. `4 marks`

```
function itemToBeFound(dataItem)

    currentPointer = startingPointer

    while currentPointer != nullPointer and list[currentPointer].data != dataItem

        currentPointer = list[currentPointer].pointer

    endwhile

    return currentPointer

endfunction
```

**13** Explain how an item of data is removed from a linked list. `3 marks`

.............................................................................................................................

.............................................................................................................................

.............................................................................................................................

.............................................................................................................................

.............................................................................................................................

## Trees

| Data can also be stored in hierarchical structures called trees. Each tree has a root node and child nodes.

**14** What is a root node? `1 mark`

.............................................................................................................................

.............................................................................................................................

**15** What is a child node? `1 mark`

.............................................................................................................................

.............................................................................................................................

The pathways that join the nodes are called branches, for example:

Pointers are used to indicate the hierarchy of the nodes.

One type of tree structure is a binary tree. A binary tree is a structure where each node can only have two child nodes. Each node therefore has the data, a left pointer and a right pointer.

To add an item of data to a sorted binary tree, the item of data is first compared to the root node. If it is greater than the root node, the right branch is followed. If it is less than the root node, the left branch is followed. This method is repeated with each node until a free space is reached and the data can be added.

**16** **Draw a binary tree to store this data set in alphabetical order:**  `4 marks`

Monkey, Elephant, Giraffe, Lion, Tiger, Penguin, Leopard, Antelope, Gorilla, Zebra, Wallaby

**17** What is a leaf node?  1 mark

........................................................................................................................................................

........................................................................................................................................................

# Graphs

A graph is a non-linear data structure that is a collection of nodes and the connections that are built between them. The nodes are sometimes known as vertices and the lines that connect two nodes are sometimes known as edges. Graphs can be used to represent many real-world problems. One scenario they are often used to represent is networks. There are two basic approaches to traversing a graph: depth-first and breadth-first.

**18** What does it mean to traverse a graph using depth-first?  1 mark

........................................................................................................................................................

........................................................................................................................................................

**19** What does it mean to traverse a graph using breadth-first?  1 mark

........................................................................................................................................................

........................................................................................................................................................

# Data searching and sorting

There may be occasions when data needs to be searched or sorted. There are several ways this can be done.

## Linear search

The most simple way to search through a set of data is to use a linear search. This is when each item of data is looked at in turn, until the item required is found.

**20** Complete the gaps in algorithm given. It is an algorithm to perform a linear search.  5 marks

```
pointer = 0

indexMax = 9

value = input("Value to find")

while ........................ < ........................ and list [pointer] != ........................ then

   pointer = pointer + 1

endwhile

if pointer >= ........................ then

   output("Item not in list")

else

   output("Item is at location" + ........................)

endif
```

# Binary search

Another type of searching algorithm is a binary search. A binary search is an example of a divide and conquer approach. It works by dividing a list of data into two sections until the value required is found.

**21** What must be done to a set of data before a binary search can be performed? `1 mark`

........................................................................................................................................................

........................................................................................................................................................

**22** Complete the gaps in the algorithm given. It is an algorithm to perform a binary search. `7 marks`

```
lowerBound = 0

upperBound = lengthOfList - 1

found = false

searchValue = input("Value to find")

while ............................... == false and upperBound != ...............................

   midpoint = round((lowerBound + upperBound)/2)

   if list[midpoint] == ............................... then

      found = true

   elseif list[...............................] < searchValue then

      lowerBound = ...............................

   else

      upperBound = ...............................

   endif

endwhile

if found == ............................... then

   print("Not in list")

else

   print("Item in position" + midpoint + "in list")
endif
```

**23** In what circumstance could a linear search be faster than a binary search? `2 marks`

........................................................................................................................................................

........................................................................................................................................................

........................................................................................................................................................

........................................................................................................................................................

........................................................................................................................................................

........................................................................................................................................................

........................................................................................................................................................

........................................................................................................................................................

# Bubble sort

A bubble sort is the simplest way to sort a data set. The current value in the list is compared to the next value in the list. If it is greater than the next value, the two values are swapped and the current value becomes the value in the next position. This occurs until the end of the list is reached. This process is repeated until the data is sorted.

A possible algorithm for a bubble sort could be:

```
listLength = indexMax

  do

    moreSwaps = false

    for x = 1 to listLength

      if list[x] > list[x + 1] then

      tempValue = list[x]

      list[x] = list[x + 1]

      list[x + 1] = tempValue

      moreSwaps = true

    endif

  until moreSwaps = false
```

**24** **How does a computer know that a data set is in order when it performs a bubble sort?** `1 mark`

..................................................................................................................................................................................

..................................................................................................................................................................................

**25** **Draw a diagram to represent how a bubble sort works. Use the data set C, F, A, B, E, D, G.** `3 marks`

# Insertion sort

A second sorting algorithm that can be used is an insertion sort. An insertion sort works by creating a new list that will then divide the data into two lists. The new list is the sorted list and the current list is the unsorted list.

The first item in the current list is made into a new list. The second item in the current list is then compared to the last item in the new list. If it is larger, it is added to the end of the new list. If it is smaller, it is compared to the previous item in the new list. This occurs until it is the larger item, where it is then inserted.

26 **Draw a diagram to represent how an insertion sort works. Use the data set 55, 24, 66, 32, 16, 47, 51, 19.**
4 marks

27 **Using pseudocode, write an algorithm that represents an insertion sort for a list of 8 values.**
5 marks

# Merge sort

A third sorting algorithm that can be used is a merge sort. A merge sort works by dividing each element in a list into a singular item. Items are then paired together and sorted. The paired lists are then paired together and sorted. This pairing process occurs until the list is a complete list again. Merge sort is also an example of a divide and conquer approach.

**28** Draw a diagram to represent how a merge sort work. Use the data set 55, 24, 66, 32, 16, 47, 51, 19.　　　　　　　　　　　　　　　　　　　　　　　　　`4 marks`

**29 a** Do you think the insertion sort or the merge sort would be quicker at sorting the data? Explain your answer.　　　　　　　　　　　　`2 marks`

.......................................................................................................................................

.......................................................................................................................................

.......................................................................................................................................

.......................................................................................................................................

**b** When might the other algorithm be quicker?　　　　　　　　　`1 mark`

.......................................................................................................................................

.......................................................................................................................................

.......................................................................................................................................

# Quicksort

A fourth sorting algorithm that can be used is a quicksort. A quicksort works by selecting an item in the list (normally the first item) and making it a pivot. This means that it becomes a single item that will be used to divide the other items into two lists. The remaining items are divided into two lists by comparing them to the pivot and placing them in a list before or after the pivot, depending on if they are smaller or greater than the pivot. A pivot is then selected from each sub-list and the process is repeated. Eventually all items in the list will become pivots and the list can them be reassembled.

**30** Draw a diagram to represent how a quicksort works. Use the data set 55, 24, 66, 32, 16, 47, 51, 19.

4 marks

**31** What is a quicksort also an example of?

1 mark

..................................................................................................................................................................

..................................................................................................................................................................

# Shortest-path algorithms

## Dijkstra's shortest-path algorithm

Dijkstra's shortest-path algorithm simply finds the shortest path between two points. Dijkstra's algorithm could be used to find the shortest path from node A to node J:

It is initially assumed that the distance from node A to every other node is infinity. This is because the node has not yet been visited to establish the distance. Once the node has been visited, the distance to the node can be recorded. For example, when nodes B and C are visited from node A, their distance can be recorded in a table:

| Node | Shortest distance from A | Previous node |
|---|---|---|
| A (C) | 0 | |
| B | ∞ 50 | A |
| C | ∞ 25 | A |
| D | ∞ | |
| E | ∞ | |
| F | ∞ | |
| G | ∞ | |
| H | ∞ | |
| I | ∞ | |
| J | ∞ | |

Once all the nodes directly connected to A have been visited and it has been established which is the closest node, then that node becomes the current node and all the nodes directly connected to that node are visited to establish their distance. The table is then updated with further values:

| Node | Shortest distance from A | Previous node |
|---|---|---|
| A | ∞ 0 | |
| B | ∞ 50 | A |
| C | ∞ 25 | A |
| D | ∞ 75 | B |
| E | ∞ 70 | C |
| F | ∞ 75 | C |
| G | ∞ 100 | E |
| H | ∞ 105 100 | E F |
| I | ∞ 130 | B |
| J | ∞ 180 160 | G I |

**32** Look at the completed table. Work backwards through the table to establish what the shortest route is.

1 mark

........................................................................................................................................................

........................................................................................................................................................

## The A* search

The A* search also finds the shortest path between two points. It does this in a more efficient way than Dijkstra's algorithm using heuristics. The heuristic used is an estimated value of the straight-line distance between the current node and the destination node. The heuristic values are shown in blue in the diagram:

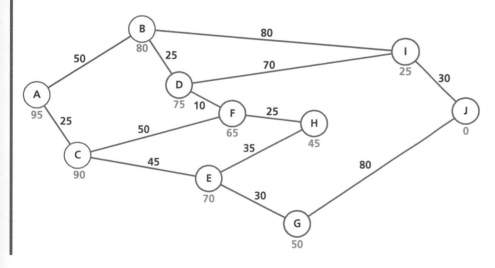

The heuristic value is added to the actual value of the distance between two connecting nodes. The algorithm is repeated in the same way as Dijkstra's but using the sum of the actual value and the heuristic value:

| Node | Path distance (g) | Heuristic distance (h) | f=g+h | Previous node |
|------|-------------------|------------------------|-------|---------------|
| A | 0 | 95 | 95 | |
| B | 50 | 80 | 130 | A |
| C | 25 | 90 | 115 | A |
| D | 75 | 75 | 150 | B |
| E | 70 | 70 | 140 | C |
| F | 75 | 65 | 140 | C |
| G | 100 | 50 | 150 | E |
| H | 100 | 45 | 145 | F |
| I | 130 | 25 | 155 | B |
| J | 180 | 0 | ~~180~~ 160 | ~~G~~ I |

## Exam-style questions

15

**34** Look at the following diagram and use Dijkstra's algorithm to find the shortest path from Node 0 to Node 7.

4 marks

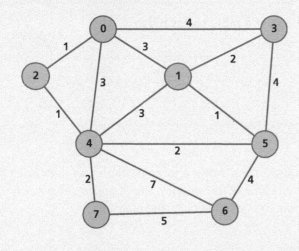

**35** Consider the following two algorithms:

1

```
def my_function(list):
    length = len(list)
    for y in range(0, length):
        for x in range(0, length - 1):
            if list[x] > list[x + 1]:
                swap = list[x]
                list[x] = list[x + 1]
                list[x + 1] = swap
```

2

```
def my_function(list):
    more = True
    length = len(list)
    counter = 0
    count = 0
    while more:
        if list[counter] > list[counter + 1]:
            swap = list[counter]
            list[counter] = list[counter + 1]
            list[counter + 1] = swap
            count = count + 1
        counter = counter + 1
        if counter == length - 1:
            if count == 0:
                more = False
            else:
                counter = 0
                count = 0
```

a  **Identify the purpose of the two algorithms.**  `1 mark`

b  **Explain the purpose of the variable 'more'.**  `2 marks`

c  **Identify the name of the value 'list' in the brackets on line 1 of the algorithm.**  `1 mark`

d  **Identify which algorithm would be more efficient and explain your choice.**  `4 marks`

**36** Explain how a queue would be stored in an array. `5 marks`

Hachette UK's policy is to use papers that are natural, renewable and recyclable products and made from wood grown in well-managed forests and other controlled sources. The logging and manufacturing processes are expected to conform to the environmental regulations of the country of origin.

Orders: please contact Hachette UK Distribution, Hely Hutchinson Centre, Milton Road, Didcot, Oxfordshire, OX11 7HH. Telephone: (44) 01235 827827. E-mail education@hachette.co.uk
Lines are open from 9 a.m. to 5 p.m., Monday to Friday. You can also order through our website: www.hoddereducation.co.uk

ISBN: 978-1-5104-3700-5

© Sarah Lawrey 2019

First published in 2019 by

Hodder Education,
An Hachette Company
Carmelite House
50 Victoria Embankment
London
EC4Y 0DZ

www.hoddereducation.co.uk

Impression number  10 9 8 7 6 5

Year        2023

Cover photo: AndSus/Fotolia

Typeset by Aptara, India

Printed in the UK

A catalogue record for this title is available from the British Library.

**HODDER** EDUCATION

t:  01235 827827
e:  education@hachette.co.uk
w:  hoddereducation.co.uk

ISBN 978-1-5104-3700-5

9 781510 437005